IMAGES
of Rail

The CHESAPEAKE and OHIO RAILWAY

Sleep like a Kitten

If you could stay awake on a Chesapeake and Ohio thru train—mind you, we say *if*—you would watch in vain for soot and cinders to trace patterns on the sheet. You would leave *untouched* the handkerchief you provided to mop your brow. You would sniff in vain for that dead air odor.... ¶ *Winter or summer*—genuine air-conditioning, built into every *Chesapeake and Ohio thru train*, makes it practically impossible to avoid sleeping like a kitten. What's more, you face the morning thoroughly *refreshed*.... ¶ Skeptical?... Then test for yourself the sleeping potency of air-conditioning. The ticket agent of *any* railroad can route you on the Chesapeake and Ohio. *Insist upon it!*

THE GEORGE WASHINGTON • THE SPORTSMAN • THE F. F. V.

All genuinely air-conditioned

Serving
WASHINGTON • PHILADELPHIA • NEW YORK • CINCINNATI • LEXINGTON
LOUISVILLE • CHICAGO • DETROIT • TOLEDO • CLEVELAND • ST. LOUIS
INDIANAPOLIS • COLUMBUS • RICHMOND • NORFOLK • NEWPORT NEWS

CHESAPEAKE and OHIO

Chessie, the Chesapeake and Ohio Railway's much-loved trademark, made her first appearance in this advertisement in the September 1933 issue of *Fortune* magazine. Within days, the railway was flooded with hundreds of requests for reprints, and a long-running ad campaign was born. In the decades since, Chessie has appeared on calenders, playing cards, drinking glasses, scarves, neckties, and a host of other items.

ON THE COVER: "No. 3 and its crew" reads a note penciled on the back of this otherwise unidentified old photograph. The Chesapeake and Ohio Railway's No. 3 was the westbound Washington-Cincinnati section of its *Fast Flying Virginian*. Debuting in 1889, the *FFV* was the C&O's first named train.

IMAGES
of Rail

The CHESAPEAKE *and* OHIO RAILWAY

James E. Casto

ARCADIA
PUBLISHING

Copyright © 2006 by James E. Casto
ISBN 978-1-5316-2636-5

Published by Arcadia Publishing
Charleston, South Carolina

Library of Congress Catalog Card Number: 2006927601

For all general information contact Arcadia Publishing at:
Telephone 843-853-2070
Fax 843-853-0044
E-mail sales@arcadiapublishing.com
For customer service and orders:
Toll-Free 1-888-313-2665

Visit us on the Internet at www.arcadiapublishing.com

The author, costumed as Collis P. Huntington, greets visitors to 1999 ceremonies marking the return of Huntington's statue to its former place of honor outside CSX Transportation's Huntington offices, located in the city's ex-passenger station. (Photograph by Charles Bowen.)

Contents

Acknowledgments		6
Introduction		7
1.	"George Washington's Railroad"	9
2.	Passenger Stations, Freight Depots, and More	23
3.	The Age of Steam	45
4.	Dawn of the Diesels	61
5.	Carrying Coal	69
6.	"The Finest Fleet of Trains in the World"	81
7.	The Greenbrier	97
8.	The Chessie Story	107
9.	Last Look	117

Acknowledgments

In 1984, I was commissioned to write a history of my hometown, Huntington, West Virginia. Collis P. Huntington founded the city of Huntington in 1871 as what was then the western terminus of his Chesapeake & Ohio Railway (C&O). As part of my research, I set out to learn as much as I could about the famed rail tycoon and the C&O.

More than 20 years and a half-dozen books later, I'm still learning.

This book contains some of what I've found over the years, along with dozens of old photographs, postcards, and items of memorabilia that I've collected. It is by no means a complete history of the C&O. Instead, it's simply an affectionate look back at what long was one of the nation's premier railroads.

I owe a lengthy list of people a debt of gratitude for assisting me in my efforts. That list includes rail fan and fellow newspaperman Bob Withers, river historian Jerry Sutphin, and Randy Cheetham, CSX Transportation regional vice president—public affairs. At the very top of the list of those due my thanks is Thomas W. Dixon Jr., chairman and president of the C&O Historical Society, who not only was generous with his advice and guidance but also loaned many of the photographs included here.

Images of Chessie and other copyrighted works of CSX are used in this book with the permission of CSX Transportation.

If this book ignites your interest in learning more about the C&O, there's a whole shelf of other informative books about it. Let me urge you to join the C&O Historical Society. Membership information is available at P.O. Box 79, Clifton Forge, VA 24422, telephone (540)862–2210 or on line at www.cohs.org.

INTRODUCTION

In its heyday, the Chesapeake and Ohio Railway proudly billed itself as "George Washington's Railroad." The C&O's premier passenger train was named the *George Washington*, and the nation's first president frequently appeared in the railway's advertisements.

George Washington died in 1799, nearly three decades before America saw its first railroad. Nevertheless, the C&O's claim to Washington as its founder had at least a thread of truth. As a young man, Washington helped survey parts of what was then this country's frontier, the vast wilderness just over the mountains from Virginia's Tidewater region. His experience convinced Washington that westward lay opportunity, and so, in 1785, he organized the James River Company, which set about linking east with west. The canals and roads built by the James River Company later became the property of the Richmond and Alleghany Railroad, which would become part of the C&O.

At its height in the 1950s and 1960s, the C&O would be the product of about 150 smaller rail lines that were incorporated into the system over the years. The first of these was the Louisa Railroad, chartered in 1836. Through successive reorganizations and name changes, the company came to be known as the Chesapeake and Ohio Railroad. Later still another reorganization would change "Railroad" to "Railway."

In 1867, the legislatures of Virginia and West Virginia enacted measures "to provide for the completion of a line or lines of railroad from the waters of the Chesapeake to the Ohio River." At the time, the rail line extended from Richmond to Covington, Virginia, a distance of 227 miles.

The all-but-bankrupt railroad desperately needed new capital to extend its track to the Ohio River, so Gen. W. C. Wickham, the C&O's president, approached Collis P. Huntington, who raised the money needed. Huntington was well known in the growing railroad industry as one of the "Big Four" partners who had constructed the Central Pacific portion of the transcontinental railroad.

In July 1869, Huntington, who assumed the C&O presidency, traveled with Wickham and Maj. H. D. Whitcomb, the C&O's chief engineer, to inspect the proposed route to the Ohio. Arriving at the river, Huntington shunned the existing communities and instead picked out a vacant tract of riverbank and there set about building a new town that would be the C&O's western terminus. Perhaps not surprisingly, he named his new town Huntington.

A wood-burning locomotive, the *Greenbrier*, was floated down the Ohio River to begin work on the western end of the railroad. Another crew pushed track eastward to Huntington. The two sets of track were linked at Hawk's Nest, West Virginia, on January 29, 1873.

A train crowded with VIPs was the first to make the 423-mile trip from Richmond to Huntington. On its return trip, the train hauled something far more important than those dignitaries: it hauled four carloads of West Virginia coal. The 23,000 tons of coal moved by the C&O that first year wouldn't even be a fraction of the incredible tonnages that would follow in the years to come.

Coal traffic—originating on a network of branch lines built to the mines—would become the lifeblood of the C&O.

While the link to his new town was under construction, Huntington looked eastward and began quietly buying up tracts of land in Newport News, Virginia, where he envisioned a busy ocean terminal. The C&O tracks were extended to Newport News in 1882, and soon West Virginia coal was flowing overseas.

Huntington saw the C&O as a potential link in a great transcontinental railroad empire, but his hopes were frustrated, and in 1888, he lost control of the C&O to the Morgan and Vanderbilt interests. Huntington would remain the westward terminus of the C&O only briefly. Soon its tracks extended westward from Huntington to Cincinnati, and a connection was also built to Lexington, Kentucky. Absorbing the Hocking Valley gave the C&O entry to Columbus and Toledo, Ohio. Still later, the railroad expanded into Indiana and on to Chicago and the Great Lakes.

Following World War I, the C&O went through several leadership changes, eventually ending up in the hands of Oris P. and Mantis J. Van Sweringen, two brothers who were Cleveland financiers. The Van Sweringens planned to combine the C&O, the Pere Marquette, the Erie, the Nickel Plate, and other lines into one giant railroad. Their plan failed. Nevertheless, the C&O ultimately emerged with control of the Pere Marquette, which operated primarily in Michigan and Ontario.

When the Great Depression forced other railroads into bankruptcy, the C&O not only survived but thrived. Even during the hard times of the Depression, the nation needed coal, and the railway prospered by providing it. It invested those profits in upgrading its roadbed and equipment, an investment that would pay off in a big way when the C&O was tasked with meeting the monumental demands of World War II.

The Depression also saw the debut of one of America's best-known trademarks: Chessie, the sleeping railroad kitten. Her initial appearance in a 1933 magazine advertisement immediately won her a legion of fans, and even today, Chessie remains popular, with her image on a vast array of items. For many years, the C&O issued Chessie calendars and was hard-pressed to keep up with the public's requests for them.

From 1942 until 1954, the C&O's chairman was the flamboyant Robert R. Young, who was determined to shake up not just the C&O but the entire railroad industry. Young launched a crusade against what he saw as mismanagement of the nation's railroads by banking interests, and he tirelessly campaigned for improved railroad passenger service. In a famous advertisement he personally wrote for the C&O, he complained: "A hog can cross the country without changing trains—but you can't." He changed the C&O's herald (logo) to "C&O for Progress" to embody his premise that the C&O would lead the rail industry to a new day.

The C&O purchased the Greenbrier in 1910 and successfully operated it for decades before it was taken over by the army for use as a military hospital during World War II. Under Young, the C&O repurchased the famed resort and lavished millions of dollars on returning it to its former splendor.

Young sought to merge the C&O with the New York Central (NYC) and, when that effort failed, instead left the C&O to become chairman of the NYC. Cleveland financier Cyrus Eaton succeeded Young as C&O chairman. Under Eaton, C&O president Walter J. Tuohy continued many of Young's modernization polices, including the railroad's reluctant switch from steam to diesel power.

In 1963, Tuohy engineered the C&O's takeover of the financially troubled Baltimore & Ohio Railroad in the first of what would become a wave of railroad mergers. Today the old C&O is part of CSX Transportation, one of the four giant railroad systems that are the result of the merger era.

One

"GEORGE WASHINGTON'S RAILROAD"

In a stirring scene, the *George Washington*, the Chesapeake and Ohio's premier passenger train, is shown leaving the nation's capital. The train's name seemed fitting for a rail line that frequently billed itself as "George Washington's Railroad," a claim based on Washington's advocacy of westward expansion and his organization in 1785 of the James River Company, a predecessor of the Chesapeake and Ohio (C&O). (Courtesy of the C&O Historical Society Collection.)

In 1784, Washington wrote Benjamin Harrison, then the governor of Virginia, and urged: "Smooth the road and make easy the way [between East and West], and see what an influx of articles will be poured upon us; how amazingly our exports will be increased . . . and how amply we shall be compensated." This portrait of Washington as a young surveyor is from Washington Irving's *Life of George Washington*.

The James River Company's ambitious plans envisioned building a canal from Richmond to the Kanawha River. Work was started in 1820 and portions of the canal were completed and put in service, but it never stretched west past Buchanan, Virginia. Halted by the Civil War, work on the canal resumed after the war, but the waterway was unable to compete with the burgeoning railroads. It ceased operations in 1880. This scene from *Harper's Weekly* shows the canal in Richmond in 1865.

The James River and Kanawha Turnpike met with more success than the company's canal. It not only reached the Kanawha River, it extended on to the Ohio, providing a rough but serviceable roadway for travelers by foot, horseback, or stagecoaches such as this. The turnpike was the primary western link for commerce between the James and the Ohio until the C&O was completed in the period 1870–1873. (Courtesy of the C&O Historical Society Collection.)

Like countless others, Connecticut storekeeper Collis P. Huntington was drawn to California by the gold rush of 1849. Unlike most, he struck it rich—not by mining gold but by mining the miners. He opened a hardware store where he sold the miners the tools and other supplies they needed, amassing a small fortune in the process. Huntington joined partners Leland Stanford, Charles Crocker, and Mark Hopkins (the "Big Four") in constructing the Central Pacific, the western leg of the transcontinental railroad. When the C&O needed money to push its tracks across the mountains and on to the Ohio River, it turned to Huntington. He supplied the money—and installed himself as C&O president.

The vintage postcards reprinted on this and the next few pages are offered to illustrate the daunting challenge faced by the C&O's crews as they pushed its tracks westward from Richmond over the mountains and across the then-new state of West Virginia. The work required construction of a number of tunnels such as this one—Mason's Tunnel on the C&O mainline near Clifton Forge, Virginia. Note the trackside bank abloom with wildflowers. A major C&O rebuilding program at the end of World War II included construction of a cut to replace the old tunnel.

The old forge and cliff from which Clifton Forge, Virginia, derived its name stand beside the C&O's double tracks in this undated postcard. Here the C&O's James River line leaves the mainline and follows along the banks of the James River to Richmond. The track, for a great part of the way, is laid on the towpath of the old James River and Kanawha Canal.

James River, C. and O. Ry. looking West from Natural Bridge Station, Va.

Fifty-one miles east of Clifton Forge on the James River line is the Natural Bridge of Virginia, one of the great wonders of the world. This postcard view was taken looking west along the James River and the C&O tracks from Natural Bridge Station.

574. MOUNTAIN SCENERY ALONG C. & O. RY., NEAR LEXINGTON, VIRGINIA.

Lexington, Virginia, home to the Virginia Military Institute (known as the "West Point of the South") and to Washington and Lee University, was reached by the C&O's James River line. Here's a glimpse of some of the spectacular mountain scenery along the C&O near Lexington.

This postcard view was taken on the C&O at Price's Bluff near Gala, Virginia. The card wasn't mailed, and so carries no postmark, but it appears to date from the early 1900s.

Price's Bluff, near Gala, Va. on line of C. and O.

Jerry's Run, Va. Jerry's Run Fill.

For many years, Jerry's Run in Virginia was the largest railroad fill in the world. The mammoth fill contained more than a million cubic yards of material. The temporary track laid around the fill while it was under construction was the scene of the C&O's worst passenger train wreck ever in 1870. A dozen people were killed when their coach slipped off the track and down the steep precipice.

14

West of Covington, Virginia, the C&O mainline ascends Alleghany Mountain, passes through the Alleghany Tunnel and emerges, as shown in this vintage postcard, at Tuckahoe, West Virginia. The state line runs through the middle of the tunnel.

Located deep in the New River Gorge near Fayette, West Virginia, Whitcomb's Boulder seems to defy gravity by the way it hangs over the C&O's tracks. A much-photographed landmark, the rock formation was named for Maj. H. D. Whitcomb, the superintendent of the old Virginia Central who would later oversee the C&O's westward expansion.

The workers who enabled the C&O to tunnel through the Alleghany Mountains were called "steel drivers" because they pounded steel drills into the rock, creating holes that were packed with dynamite to blast it loose. It was dangerous work that required incredible strength. To pass the time, the men would sing, and their songs weaved the legend of John Henry, said to be the strongest of them all, even beating a steam drill the company brought in. In 1996, the U.S. Postal Service issued this stamp honoring John Henry.

John Henry may or may not have been a real person; the experts disagree. But there's no disputing the fact that he has a suitably impressive statue. Here a special train carrying the larger-than-life statue makes its way through the Great Bend Tunnel, which he is said to have helped dig. Erected in 1972, the bronze statute stands eight feet tall and weighs approximately two and a half tons. It was placed near Talcott, West Virginia, in a small park on State Route 3/12 overlooking the tunnel. (Photograph by Thomas W. Dixon Jr., courtesy of the C&O Historical Society Collection.)

In 1930–1932, the C&O constructed a second tunnel adjacent to the Great Bend Tunnel. The new tunnel is shown here with an unidentified visitor in an undated photograph. Until 1974, the mile-long tunnels were used in tandem, with one carrying eastbound train traffic and the other westbound traffic. In that year, the old tunnel was closed, and all traffic now passes through the new tunnel.

The Shoo Fly Tunnel and the C&O's rugged New River line are shown in this vintage view. Shortly after the C&O arrived, coal was discovered in the New River Gorge, and mining towns quickly sprang up. When the coal played out, the towns were just as quickly abandoned. The ruins of many former coal tipples and coke ovens can still be seen from the tracks. The Shoo Fly Tunnel was abandoned in 1941.

Although West Virginia is synonymous with coal, the state also has been home to a thriving timber industry. Shown here is the Pocahontas County town of Cass, built in 1902 and named after Jacob Cass, an official of the timber company that started the community. Narrow-gauge locomotives and flatcars were used to haul the fallen logs down from Cheat Mountain. They then were transferred to the C&O for their trip to market. Today the old narrow-gauge railroad is one of the state's most popular tourist destinations.

Here's a vintage view of Sharp's Tunnel and the Greenbrier River bridge on the Greenbrier Division of the C&O at Harter, about nine miles east of Marlinton, West Virginia. Much of the West Virginia timber hauled on the division ended up at the West Virginia Pulp and Paper Company's giant mill at Covington, Virginia.

The overlook at Hawk's Nest State Park provides a breathtaking view of West Virginia's New River Gorge and the C&O's tracks 585 feet below. This heavily retouched postcard of visitors taking in the view dates from the 1940s.

19

When Collis P. Huntington established the new town of Huntington as the western terminus of the C&O, work immediately started on extensive railroad facilities there. The C&O's annual report for 1872 announced: "One fourth of the engine house is completed and occupied; the workshops are in progress; the machine and car shops are completed for 120 feet; the blacksmiths' for 60 feet. A fireproof oil house, brick office [and] house for a stationary engine have been built."

Here's an undated, early view of a group of unidentified workers at the C&O's Huntington shop. Today the shop, although much altered over the years, remains a busy place and a major employer in Huntington.

Collis P. Huntington and other backers organized the Ensign Manufacturing Company in Huntington in 1872. The plant's first products were railcar wheels, but soon it began manufacturing wooden railcars. By the mid 1890s, the Ensign plant was turning out more than 4,000 railcars a year, including many—such as this gondola built in 1897—for the C&O. In 1899, Ensign was one of more than a dozen car builders consolidated into the American Car and Foundry Company (now ACF Industries).

In its early years, the C&O provided connecting service between Huntington and Portsmouth via packet boats, including the *Fleetwood* and *Bostona* (shown here). Note the C&O name inscribed on the paddlewheel housing. The packet boats carried both freight and passengers, who paid $2 for the trip. The business was discontinued with completion of the C&O's Cincinnati Division in 1888. (From the Steamboat Photograph Collection of G. H. "Jerry" Sutphin.)

John's Rock on the C. and O., near Ashland, Ky.

This undated vintage postcard shows a passenger train at John's Rock on the C&O near Ashland, Kentucky. In 1907, when the C&O learned that other railroads—chiefly the Baltimore and Ohio and the Hocking Valley—were showing interest in the untapped coal deposits known to be in Eastern Kentucky, it moved to consolidate its several Kentucky lines. The resulting 438 miles of track formed the C&O of Kentucky. The area was officially designated the railway's Big Sandy Division in 1914.

THE C. & O. NORTHERN RAILWAY BRIDGE, PORTSMOUTH, OHIO

In 1914–1917, the C&O spanned the Ohio River at Portsmouth with a bridge built to carry its new connection from Russell, Kentucky, north to Columbus, Ohio. The resulting span was constructed to carry the heaviest weight of any bridge ever erected.

Two

Passenger Stations, Freight Depots, and More

Topped by an imposing clock tower, Main Street Station in Richmond, Virginia, was constructed as a union station for the C&O and the Seaboard Air Line Railroad. This old postcard view of the station shows at left a portion of the station's 550-foot-long train shed, a clear arch span with no intermediate supports. No ceremonies were held when the station opened on November 27, 1901. Nevertheless, thousands of people showed up that day, many of them no doubt curious to see what $2 million—the station's reported cost—would buy.

In his *Virginia Railway Depots*, Donald R. Traser wrote that increased traffic, longer trains, and heavier locomotives rendered the Richmond station "obsolete almost from the beginning," but much-debated plans for its expansion or renovation went nowhere, and the post-World War II decline in passenger traffic made the point moot.

Collis P. Huntington realized that the C&O needed a deep-water port, so in 1882, he extended its tracks down the Virginia peninsula from Richmond to the great natural harbor at Newport News on Hampton Roads. This handsome station welcomed its first passengers on December 1 of that year. The station's clock tower was removed in the 1920s. The station itself was demolished in 1949 and replaced with a small brick structure. Later Amtrak would build its own station four miles up the line.

CHESAPEAKE & OHIO FERRY BOAT, BETWEEN NEWPORT NEWS AND NORFOLK, VA.

Trains arriving at the Newport News station stopped at the adjacent shed/pier, where passengers bound for Norfolk transferred to this steam ferry, the *Virginia*, for the ride across Hampton Roads. The C&O abandoned the ferry service in 1950 and retired the 1902-era *Virginia*. After that, passengers were shuttled between Newport News and Norfolk by bus until 1971, when Amtrak discontinued Norfolk service altogether.

The C&O was a huge presence in early Newport News, with Huntington and his associates building various business interests through their Newport News Shipbuilding and Dry Dock Company. The C&O itself found that it had to continually expand its facilities at Newport News as business boomed and the demand for export coal increased. This postcard, postmarked in 1910, shows a four-masted sailing ship at C&O Pier 4.

25

To handle the important grain and flour trade, Huntington formed the C&O Grain Elevator Company and leased this elevator from the Hazeltine family. The big elevator's capacity was 1.5 million bushels. A smaller elevator was constructed in Richmond. The photograph of C&O Pier 4 shown at the top of this page was shot from the Newport News elevator.

The C&O not only shuttled passengers across Hampton Roads, it did the same with freight cars. Big, tug-powered, barge-like car floats like this one left the C&O's terminal at Newport News on the north (peninsula) side of the harbor and brought freight to a C&O depot in downtown Norfolk at Brooke Avenue. Each float could accommodate more than a dozen freight cars.

This vintage postcard offers a bird's-eye view of the C&O freight depot in Norfolk. The C&O offices and facilities are in the two-story building just left of the card's center. At the right of the card is a giant tank that was used to store molasses until shipment. The tank was demolished in the late 1960s. Portsmouth, Virginia, can be seen across the Elizabeth River.

Lee Hall is now within the city limits of Newport News but once enjoyed heavy military traffic to and from nearby Fort Eustis. This shot of the old station dates from 1978, some years after the end of passenger service in 1971.

C. & O. DEPOT, WILLIAMSBURG, VA.

The C&O's first station in Williamsburg, Virginia, was a two-story frame building. Anticipating increased traffic for the Jamestown Exposition of 1907, the C&O replaced it with a new brick station. Designed in the Colonial Revival style, it is reported to have cost $14,098 to build. In 1935, after the Rockefeller restoration of Williamsburg began, the railroad built a third station at a new site about half a mile west of the original location.

In 1872, *Scribner's Monthly* published an account of a train trip along the C&O, and in it, writer Jed Hotchkiss (famed as Gen. Stonewall Jackson's mapmaker) described how, when the train stopped at Gordonsville, passengers would lean out the windows to buy fried chicken and other foodstuffs. This woodcut accompanied the article.

For many years, the C&O and the Virginia Midland (later the Southern Railway) were partners in a union station in Charlottesville, Virginia, but in 1905, the C&O built this imposing station, the first of nine such Greek Revival stations that the railway would erect. This 1973 photograph shows the street side of the structure. (Photograph by Thomas W. Dixon Jr., courtesy of the C&O Historical Society Collection.)

The C&O crosses the Blue Ridge at Afton, Virginia, following the line of the old Blue Ridge Railroad laid out by Col. Claudius Crozet and passing through the little community named for him. This trackside view of the Crozet station was shot in 1977. (Photograph by Thomas W. Dixon Jr., courtesy of the C&O Historical Society Collection.)

The Virginia Central, a C&O predecessor, built a passenger station in Staunton, Virginia, in 1854. Burned during the Civil War, it was rebuilt after the war. A second station was built later. Still later, in 1906, it was replaced by this masonry structure. The maker of this vintage postcard destroyed the printing plates for it and stamped that fact across the front, but even so, we can still enjoy the view of this handsome old station.

The passenger platform at Staunton was shaped in a graceful arc that looked more like a classic Greek temple than a railroad station. Reporting that the new station was ready to open, the *Charlottesville Daily Progress* of April 4, 1906, wrote: "The station is equipped with all the modern conveniences, and is a credit to Staunton." The station would long be an important point on the C&O. The adjacent American Hotel was one of the places where C&O trains stopped for meals before dining cars were added.

The C&O's Craig Valley Branch connected with the railway's mainline at Eagle Rock, Virginia, seven miles east of Clifton Forge, and served 26 miles of line south of there. It was abandoned in 1961. The Eagle Rock station is shown here in an undated photograph.

The Virginia Central Railroad reached what is now Clifton Forge in 1857 and called it the Jackson River Station. The railroad's name choice didn't stick. The Gladys Inn was built in 1896 and served as both a hotel and passenger station. It is shown here in a postcard postmarked 1910. Next to it stood a railroad YMCA, one of a half-dozen built along the C&O for use of its employees. The railroad constructed a freight yard and large shops at Clifton Forge. Today it is home to the C&O Historical Society.

Clifton Forge was strategically located between the steep grades of the C&O's Mountain Subdivision and Alleghany Subdivision and the water-level James River line. Here locomotives of different power could be substituted and traffic for the three different lines could be separated and classified. Second in size only to the C&O's sprawling yards in Russell, Kentucky, Clifton Forge was always a busy place. Why this vintage postcard view shows only two lonely looking cabooses is, alas, an unsolved mystery.

Covington, Virginia, was the junction of the Hot Springs Branch of the C&O to the Homestead Hotel, some 25 miles distant. In the 1930s, as many as six trains a day carried guests to and from the famed resort. The Hot Springs Branch was abandoned in 1972, after the end of passenger service. This passenger station, erected in 1906, was the third to serve Covington, long home to one of the nation's largest paper mills.

West of Covington, the C&O mainline ascends Alleghany Mountain, passes through Alleghany Tunnel, and emerges at Tuckahoe, West Virginia. From there it continues to White Sulphur Springs and the Greenbrier resort, then on to Ronceverte. "Isn't this a good looking little depot?" asked the writer of the message on the back of this postcard, mailed in 1918. Built just three years earlier, the Ronceverte station was unusual in style, with its upper floor constituting offices.

From Ronceverte, the line follows the flow of the Greenbrier River westward to Alderson, West Virginia. This vintage photograph was taken July 4, 1917, by a photographer standing atop a C&O work train. A holiday parade can be seen crossing the tracks in the background. (Original nitrate negative from the collection of Thomas W. Dixon Jr., courtesy of the C&O Historical Society Collection.)

33

Today Alderson is best known as the site of a federal prison for women whose "guests" have included Tokyo Rose and Martha Stewart. Here's a view of the Alderson station from the cab of an E-8 leading No. 4, the *Sportsman*, into town on a summer day in 1967. The train's arrival didn't cause the stir it once did but was still, even in the twilight of the passenger era, an important event in the town's daily life. (Photograph by Thomas W. Dixon Jr.)

Hinton was the C&O's West Virginia counterpart of Clifton Forge in Virginia, serving as the point of transition between the mountainous Alleghany Subdivision to the east and the rugged New River Subdivision to the west. At its height, Hinton had a 17-engine roundhouse, freight depot, services facilities, two freight yards, and this passenger station, originally built in 1892 and added to over the years. On the hill just above the station was the railroad YMCA, where crews stayed during layovers.

In the post–World War II era, the C&O planned to build a number of art deco passenger stations, but this one at Prince was the only one actually constructed. Still used by Amtrak, the modern station looks totally out of place in its rural setting.

Although tiny in population, Thurmond was a strategic town for the C&O, serving as a hub for the extensive New River mining operations. The town attracted visitors by the score, as attested by this c. 1915 postcard showing the crowded platform at its passenger station. Some came on business. Others came seeking a good time in the many saloons, dance halls, and houses of ill repute located in the adjacent community of Glen Jean. Founder William Dabney Thurmond wouldn't allow such unwholesome activity in his town.

35

Here is a 1935 view of the C&O station at Thurmond. Today the old station has been restored by the National Park Service as part of its New River Gorge National River and is a popular spot for rail fans and other visitors. (Photograph by William Monypeny, courtesy of the C&O Historical Society Collection.)

This station, built in 1894 at Fire Creek, West Virginia, was a good example of C&O architecture. The downstairs accommodated both passengers and freight. Locating the signal tower upstairs in the same structure made efficient use of this site on the edge of the New River. (Courtesy of the C&O Historical Society Collection.)

The C&O emerges from the New River Gorge at Gauley Bridge, where the New joins the Gauley to form the Kanawha River. The tracks then follow the south side of the Kanawha to Montgomery and on to Charleston. This handsome brick station at Montgomery was built primarily to serve college students attending the West Virginia Institute of Technology.

When the C&O was constructed through Charleston, West Virginia, the tracks were laid on the south side of the Kanawha River while the city developed on the river's north side. Thus passengers had to ride a river ferry to and from the station. Construction of the city's South Side Bridge removed that necessity. The Charleston C&O station, erected in 1907, was unusual for both its large size and its two-story design. Amtrak still uses it as a stop. The old building also houses a restaurant and offices.

Twelve miles west of Charleston, at St. Albans, the Coal River Branch connects, linking the mainline to the region's coalfields. The C&O located a major yard and terminal at Danville, 35 miles up the branch from St. Albans. This shot of the Danville station is dated 1977.

The C&O's first station in the newly created town of Huntington was built in 1872, even before the rail line was completed between Huntington and Richmond. This postcard is dated 1911 and offers a good view of the ornate structure.

In 1913, the C&O constructed a handsome new Huntington passenger station of Georgian design that CSX Transportation continues to use for offices. In 1924, the Huntington family erected a statue of the late rail tycoon in front of the station. The statue by Gutson Borglum, the sculptor of Mount Rushmore, quickly became a city landmark.

In 1977, when the former Baltimore and Ohio (B&O) passenger station and freight depot in Huntington were turned into a restaurant/retail complex, Huntington's statue was moved there. One wonders what the often blunt-spoken rail baron would have said about being memorialized at a rival railroad station. In 1999, at the request of CSX, the statue was returned to its original site. Here it is during its "exile" at the former B&O station. (Photograph by the author.)

Seven miles west of Huntington, the C&O crossed the mainline of the old Norfolk and Western Railway (N&W) at Kenova, West Virginia. A two-level union passenger station handled the C&O trains on its lower level and the N&W on the upper level. Kenova was also a junction with the B&O's Ohio River Division.

Leaving West Virginia, the C&O crossed the Big Sandy River into Kentucky, reaching first Catlettsburg and then Ashland, where this large two-story stone passenger station was built.

In 1925, the C&O replaced the old Ashland station with this imposing red brick structure. Its three floors housed the station, division offices, dispatchers, and other offices. For many years, Ashland was the busiest C&O-only station on the line. It was here that trains coming in from the east were broken up and sections sent to Cincinnati, Detroit, and Louisville. In 1982, the former station was converted for use as a bank.

Cincinnati was the western terminus of the C&O from 1888 until 1910. With terminal space short, local passenger trains and freights were terminated at a makeshift facility. Name trains used Central Union Station, shown here, until 1933, when the city's grand new station was built.

41

Completed in 1933, the imposing Cincinnati Union Terminal was a masterpiece of art deco architecture and one of the last grand railroad stations built. Constructed at a cost of more than $40 million, it was designed to handle nearly 250 trains a day but never saw more than half that number, even during the busy war years.

This 1952 postcard shows the lavishly decorated concourse at Cincinnati Union Terminal, which was jointly owned by the C&O and a half-dozen other railroads. From here, the C&O sent through cars and passengers to Chicago, St. Louis, and Indianapolis. Today the former terminal is home to a museum complex. The massive rotunda survives, but the grand concourse is gone.

In 1834, before a single mile of railroad existed anywhere in Ohio, U.S. representative John Chaney proposed construction of the Hocking Valley Railroad from Lancaster to the Ohio River. When the Hocking Valley (HV) became a reality in the 1860s, it prospered from the start, primarily from hauling coal. That made it a natural fit with the C&O. The Hocking Valley was merged into the C&O in 1930, and the C&O name went up on stations such as this one at Lancaster, located roughly 30 miles from Columbus. This photograph is undated but appears to be from the 1970s.

In 1910, the C&O purchased the bankrupt Chicago, Cincinnati, and Louisville Railroad, which had been built diagonally across Indiana. Initially the C&O called it the Chesapeake & Ohio Railway of Indiana. Later it became simply the railroad's Chicago Division. Here's a shot of the C&O station at Peru, Indiana, in 1941. (Photograph by Bill Swartz.)

Imposing Union Station in Washington, D.C., was built and owned by the Pennsylvania Railroad and the Baltimore & Ohio but was important to the operations of a number of other railroads, including the C&O. From its opening in 1907 to the post-war decline of rail passenger service, it was one of the busiest passenger stations in the world. During World War II, it welcomed as many as 200,000 passengers a day.

First unsuccessfully remodeled as a visitor center that failed to draw many visitors, Washington's Union Station was revamped again in 1988, this time as a shopping complex. Today a restaurant and bar are located where decades of passengers patiently sat on these hard wooden benches. The ornate station remains a busy transit hub served by Amtrak, commuter lines, and the Washington Metro subway system.

Three

THE AGE OF STEAM

It took rugged power to haul long trains of coal out of Appalachia, and in the era of steam power, the C&O boasted some of the most powerful locomotives ever built. A good example is the Allegheny Class H-8 2-6-6-6. Three H-8s—Nos. 1616, 1607, and 1605—pose at Clifton Forge, Virginia, in 1942, shortly after their delivery from Lima Locomotive Works. (Courtesy of the C&O Historical Society Collection.)

C&O No. 66 was one of two engines operating between Huntington, West Virginia, and Cincinnati, Ohio, in the late 1880s. Engineer Arch Snedegar (standing at right) came to Huntington along with two older brothers from Jackson, Ohio. All were C&O men. Information regarding the C&O's earliest locomotives, especially those it inherited from its predecessor railroads, is sketchy.

In the mid-19th century, the American 4-4-0 was the most popular and most widely used locomotive in the nation. Not surprisingly, it was well represented in the early C&O inventory. No. 76, shown here, was built by Schenectady in 1899 and remained on the job until the mid-1920s.

Built by Baldwin in 1900, this Class C-3 0-6-0 switcher carried a half-dozen different numbers over the first half of its long life. It was finally designated 15 in C&O's system-wide renumbering of 1924. She spent her last years working out of Parsons Yard in Columbus, Ohio, and was retired in 1951.

Hocking Valley No. 89, built by American Locomotive Company (ALCO)-Brooks in 1912, became C&O F-13 No. 89. At the time of the C&O takeover, these were the HV's newest and largest passenger locomotives. Shown here at Logan, Ohio, in an undated photograph, No. 89 was retired in 1932. (Courtesy of the C&O Historical Society Collection.)

In 1925, in the C&O's first large order for switchers of a standardized design, Lima delivered 10 engines. They were given road numbers 100 through 109. In 1948, when the C&O was faced with making room on its roster for Pere Marquette diesels with those numbers, the 0-8-0 switchers were re-numbered 60 to 69. This 1938 photograph shows No. 103 at Clifton Forge, Virginia.

The far-more-powerful ten-wheeler or 4-6-0 type locomotive was the next logical step up from the popular American type. Beginning in 1871, the C&O would eventually purchase more than 150 ten-wheelers. No. 127 was one of four purchased in 1889 to haul the C&O's first named passenger train, the *Fast Flying Virginian*.

When the C&O acquired the Hocking Valley, it inherited 10 Consolidation Class G-3 2-8-0 engines numbered 150 to 159 that had been built by ALCO-Brooks in 1910. The C&O retained those numbers. One of the 10 was retired in 1934 and another in 1935. The remaining engines continued in local and work-train service until 1949, when they were scrapped. No. 156 is shown here at Covington, Kentucky, in 1939.

Called the Pacific because its design was first delivered to the Missouri Pacific, the Class F 4-6-2 debuted with the C&O in 1902 and quickly became a mainstay of its locomotive fleet. No. 169, shown in an undated photograph with workers at Hinton, West Virginia, was one of 27 engines that made up the initial F-15 class of Pacifics. All had been retired by 1952.

Beginning in 1930, the C-16 0-8-0 became the backbone of the C&O's switching fleet. Here is No. 202, as shown in an advertisement by the Locomotive Firebox Company in *Railway Age*. In 1954, 18 of the study C-16s, no longer needed with the arrival of diesel switchers, managed to escape the scrap yard when the C&O donated them to the Korean National Railway.

The fireman stokes up No. 223, an American Class A 4-4-0, before leaving Catlettsburg, Kentucky, in 1920. Just visible behind the tender is the overhanging roof of an open-vestibule wooden coach. Built by Schenectady in 1892, she was retired in 1926. (Courtesy of the C&O Historical Society Collection.)

Atlantic A-16 No. 276 is shown with a local train at the Huntington, West Virginia, passenger station in an undated photograph. The C&O received its first Atlantic 4-4-2 types in 1902 and eventually acquired 20 of them. They began heading for the scrap yard in the early 1930s, with No. 276 scrapped in 1939.

Built by Baldwin in 1902, this Class F-11 ten-wheeler was originally used in passenger service and was still operating as a road engine in 1950, hauling mixed trains between Eagle Rock and New Castle, Virginia. Retired in 1951, it was given a fancy makeover the following year for centennial festivities in Logan, West Virginia. It last ran under steam in 1969, under lease to the Toledo, Lake Erie, and Western Railway, a tourist operator. It is shown here at the B&O Railroad Museum, where it was placed in 1975.

By 1899, the C&O's traffic had grown to the point where larger locomotives were required. To meet that need, the Richmond Locomotive Works built the Consolidation Class G-6 2-8-0, which at the time was the most powerful engine acquired by the C&O. Over the next 17 years, the railway would purchase 335 G-6s. No. 419 is shown at Kenova, West Virginia, in 1909.

Shown at Toledo, Ohio, in May 1932, C&O No. 438 was one of the original Pacific Class F-15 4-6-2 locomotives delivered between 1902 and 1911. Originally numbered 147 through 173, they were extensively rebuilt and renumbered 430 through 456.

In 1923, the Richmond Locomotive Works delivered six more large Pacific locomotives that were given road numbers 188 through 193. In the system-wide renumbering the next year, they were given numbers 480 through 485. After an extensive rebuilding at the railway's Huntington Shops in 1930–1931, they were given new, larger tenders. Here's Pacific No. 482 looking mighty spiffy after its rebuild. Note the big C&O monogram on the tender.

Hudson Class L-2 No. 305 is shown new at Baldwin Locomotive Works in 1942. The C&O used the heavy, high horsepower 4-6-4 locomotives on its name trains. When the passenger diesels started arriving, the Hudsons were hit hard. Deemed unsuitable for freight work, they were finished. No. 305 was scrapped in 1955.

In the early 1930s, the C&O realized it needed new passenger power if its trains were to keep their tight schedules. The answer was the Greenbrier Class J 4-8-4, built by Lima Locomotive Works. Eventually a dozen Greenbriers were built, including No. 610, shown here crossing the Hampton Creek (Virginia) Bridge. The coming of the diesels saw Greenbriers shifted first to freight duty, then to storage. A coal boom in 1955 saw several, including the 610, returned to service but only briefly; then it was off to the scrap yard.

The only surviving locomotive of the Hocking Valley Railway is C&O No. 701, which was originally HV No. 701. The C&O used the sturdy engine, built by ALCO-Richmond in 1911, in various chores until 1940, when she was assigned to the Clifton Forge–Hot Springs run, where she worked the next 12 years before being retired in 1952. Rescued from the scrap yard, she was restored and placed on display at Covington, the city where the Hot Springs Branch once left the mainline.

From 1903 to 1907, the ALCO-Richmond Works built more than 200 Consolidation Class G-7 2-8-0 engines for the C&O. Over the years, they were to be true workhorses for the railroad. After being bumped from mainline chores by newer engines, they continued to perform switching duties. The demands of World War II extended the old engines' life, but by 1953, the last of them were gone. Here, in an undated photograph, is Consolidation G-7 No. 835 with local train No. 157 at Wheelwright, Kentucky.

In 1909, the C&O took delivery from ALCO-Richmond of 50 G-9 Consolidation 2-8-0 engines. In the 1924 renumbering, they were designated Nos. 1010 to 1059. Nearly all of them remained in service until the coming of diesel power. The last one, the 1031, went to the scrap yard in 1961. Shown here in Russell, Kentucky, in 1953 is engine No. 1041.

Everything's big in Texas, and maybe that's why the name "Texas" stuck with this 2-10-4 design first built for the Texas and Pacific by Lima. The C&O bought 30 of the big engines, taking delivery of the first, No. 3000, in 1930. This photograph shows engine No. 3002 at Fostoria, Ohio, in 1946. Between 1948 and 1953, all 30 were sold for scrap.

Built in 1926 by the American Locomotive Company in Richmond, Virginia, K-3A Mikado No. 2328 was one of the last engines built for the C&O in Richmond. The hard-working Mikados could be found throughout the C&O system. On level routes, one engine was sufficient to roll a hotshot freight, but over the mountains, they were doubleheaded, while a third engine sometimes pushed from behind. The "Mikes" were retired and eventually scrapped as the diesels began to arrive. Sadly no example of a C&O Mikado survives.

In 1948, with the optimism that characterized its postwar decision making, the C&O ordered 25 new Mallet H-6 freight locomotives to take over coal-hauling duties. The following year, when labor unrest slashed coal production—and the C&O's revenues—the railroad cancelled 15 of the 2-6-6-2 engines. The remaining 10, numbered 1300 to 1309, were delivered later that year and proved to be the last steam locomotives built by Baldwin for a U.S. railroad. No. 1309 is now part of the collection at the B&O Railroad Museum in Baltimore, Maryland, and No. 1308, shown here, is on display in Huntington, West Virginia. (Photograph by the author.)

Like its sister locomotives, C&O Mallet No. 1308 spent her brief career working out of Peach Creek in the West Virginia coalfields. She is now the centerpiece of the Huntington Railroad Museum, owned and operated by the Collis P. Huntington Railroad Historical Society, Inc. In 2003, she was named to the National Register of Historic Places. (Photograph by the author.)

Weighing nearly 600 tons and stretching 125 feet long, the C&O's mammoth H-8 Allegheny 2-6-6-6 was one of the most powerful steam locomotives ever built. Lima Locomotive Works built 60 of the giants. Today only two survive. One, No. 1601, is on display at the Henry Ford Museum at Dearborn, Michigan. The other, No. 1604, shown here, is at the B&O Railroad Museum in Baltimore, Maryland.

In 1943, when the C&O needed new locomotives, wartime restrictions stipulated the use of an already proven design, a 2-8-4 already in service on the Erie, Nickel Plate, and Pere Marquette. The C&O, however, did bestow a distinctive name on its new purchases. They were called the Kanawha type, in honor of the river the C&O mainline follows for so many miles. Here is a dramatic night shot of K-4 No. 2718 in the yard at Russell, Kentucky, in July 1945. (Courtesy of the C&O Historical Society Collection.)

C&O switchers Nos. 35, 36, and 37 (shown here) were steam powered but in a very unusual fashion. The three were built by H. K. Porter Company in 1949 for use in Charleston, West Virginia, chemical plants, where the explosive atmosphere precluded the use of a firebox or boiler. The solution was a reservoir of steam supplied by the plant's heating system.

In 1946, No. 490, built as a Pacific F-19 in 1926, was taken to the railway's Huntington Shops, stripped down to its boiler shell, and rebuilt as a streamliner designated Class L-1. The plan was to use No. 490 and her sister streamliners to haul the Newport News and Louisville sections of C&O's classy new passenger train, the *Chessie*. The new train failed to become a reality, and the L-1s were never used as intended. They were put to scattered use over the next few years and then retired. No. 490 is now at the B&O Railroad Museum in Baltimore, Maryland.

Four

Dawn of the Diesels

Before succumbing to the lure of diesel power, the C&O tried other ideas. One, as noted in the previous chapter, was streamlining old steam locomotives. An even bolder attempt to stave off the spread of the diesels was C&O's No. 500, the first coal-burning, steam, turbine-electric locomotive ever built and the largest passenger locomotive in the world. It was more than 154 feet long, including its water tender, and had a rated top speed of 100 miles per hour. Unfortunately the ill-fated locomotive never lived up to its billing, and the C&O quietly abandoned the project.

Here is another view of C&O's steam turbine, this one a painting done for the August 1948 cover of *Railroad Magazine*. Artist Frederick Blakeslee shows the 500 at a coaling station. Three of the steam turbine locomotives were built, numbered 500, 501, and 502. They saw use mostly between Clifton Forge and Charlottesville in Virginia. That streamlined coal dock was one of two especially built for the new locomotive.

The old Pere Marquette Railway in Michigan and Canada was the C&O's proving ground for diesel power. The C&O essentially controlled the Pere Marquette (PM) from the 1920s on and, in 1947, finally merged it into the main system. The PM bought its first diesel in 1939, logically enough from General Motors' Electro-Motive Division (EMD), since General Motors was one of the line's biggest shippers. In 1946, the PM inaugurated the nation's first postwar streamliners, powered by EMD E7 passenger diesels. Here is PM E7 No. 102, one of the first two to be placed in service. It's shown rounding a curve with a string of lightweight coaches.

The PM had many miles of branch line with light rail that could accommodate only the lightest of locomotives, so perhaps not surprisingly it was first in line to buy EMD's new BL2 road switcher, designed to combine the visibility of a switcher with the power of a road engine. When the first BL2 was delivered in 1948, the PM had been part of the C&O for a year, so it came with "Chesapeake & Ohio" lettered across the side, the first diesel ever to carry the C&O name. Shown is a later BL2, No. 1841.

In 1949, the C&O took delivery of two of these unusual-looking TR3 switchers for use in the yards at Russell, Kentucky. Made up of one cab-equipped unit and two cab-less boosters, they immediately were dubbed the "cow and two calves" and "herds" by the crews. Shown here at the EMD factory is No. 6500, an exact twin to No. 6501. C&O proved to be EMD's only customer for the unusual locomotives.

This E7 was originally one of the Pere Marquette's diesels, No. 107. It was renumbered C&O No. 4514 in 1962. Four years later, it was sold to the Louisville and Nashville, which used its motors to repower switchers.

The C&O's first order of F7s was intended to dieselize the line from Cincinnati to Chicago. The C&O purchased each of its F7s as a matched trio, with two A units and one B unit in the middle. In their first few years, they were in fact operated in that fashion. Eventually the trios were split up and ultimately used with other models. Here is an F7 trio shortly after its delivery in 1950. Note the coaling tower in the background. (Courtesy of the C&O Historical Society Collection.)

The EMD GP7 debuted in 1950 with an order for 20 units for use on Pere Marquette trains. Orders for large quantities for the C&O quickly followed. The GP7 and the later GP9, known to their crews as "Geeps," were real workhorses, with many remaining in service into the 1980s. GP7 No. 5745, built as part of a 1951–1952 order, was already 20 years old when pictured at Grand Blanc, Michigan, in 1971. She was finally retired and sold for scrap in 1986.

This veteran C&O GP7, No. 5838, was built in 1952. Wrecked and sold in 1973, she was rebuilt as a GP8.

Here is another GP7, No. 5882. Built in 1953, she is shown at Walbridge, Ohio, in 1980. She was scrapped in 1983.

When the C&O deemed it was time to replace its GP7s, it stuck with General Motor's Electro Motive Division. EMD's GP9 was to prove every bit as hardworking and durable as its GP7. No. 5915, shown here at Muncie, Indiana, in 1960, was built in 1954 and was in service until 1978.

With their affiliation in 1963, much of the C&O's surplus first generation diesel power was transferred to the B&O. This GP9, No. 6124, was built in 1956 and was still wearing the C&O's colors when photographed in Toledo, Ohio, in 1965. She was transferred to the B&O in 1968.

The C&O's SD18s, numbered 7300 through 7318 and built by EMD in 1963, originally were used in mainline freight service but soon were assigned to heavy yard switching duties at Russell, Kentucky. Here is No. 7303 at Russell in 1981. Most of the C&O's SD18s were either scrapped or sold to short-line carriers in the mid-1980s.

Five

CARRYING COAL

The C&O lavished considerable attention (and money) on its passenger service, with such famed trains as the *George Washington*. It hauled a wide range of cargo—timber, foodstuffs, and thousands of products from hundreds of factories. But the C&O's name will forever be linked with one product—coal—and scenes such as this one, showing a loaded coal train rounding a curve on the C&O's Piney Creek Branch in West Virginia. This undated photograph was widely used in C&O publicity. (Courtesy of the C&O Historical Society Collection.)

COAL MINE PORTAL NEAR WHITESVILLE, W. VA.

An undated postcard shows the portal of the Glogora Coal Company mine near Whitesville, West Virginia. This is a typical "drift" mine, where the shaft goes into a coal seam horizontally, meaning the miners can travel directly into the mine on low-slung cars generally called "buggies" rather than being lowered vertically. Look closely, and you can see two miners lounging to the left of the portal or "mouth."

Electric Mining Machine in Elkhorn (Ky.) Coal Mine, Consolidation Coal Co., Inc., Baltimore, U. S. A.

It may look primitive now, but this machine was the latest thing when it replaced the traditional pick and shovel at this Consolidation Coal Company mine at Elkhorn City, Kentucky. The rich eastern Kentucky coalfields were tapped by the C&O's Big Sandy Subdivision, constructed in the period 1902–1906.

Postmarked in 1909, this card shows the hillside tipple of a mine at Boomer near Montgomery in Fayette County, West Virginia. No railcars are visible, but the rail tracks can clearly be seen running across the bottom of the card.

The caption on this undated postcard reads "Coal Tipple, Charleston, W.Va.," but more than likely it is not a scene from Charleston proper. It's probably from a few miles away in rural Kanawha County, perhaps the Cabin Creek area, home to a number of mines served by the C&O. Tipples were so named because they were the place where loaded cars emerging from the mine were tipped over and dumped into waiting railroad hoppers below. Later, modern tipples cleaned and sorted the coal as well.

71

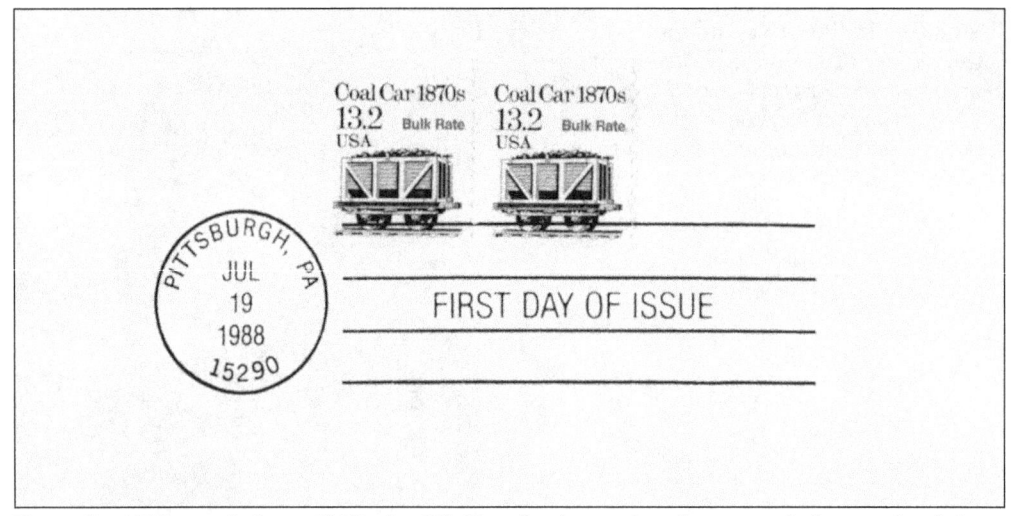

From the 1870s until about 1900, the C&O and other railroads operated thousands of these five-ton wooden hopper cars generally called "jimmies" that were used to haul coal from mine to market. The cars' wheels were attached directly to the frame, making them susceptible to frequent derailments. Still, trains of 100 or more of these little hoppers were common until bigger and better coal cars came along. The U.S. Postal Service honored the little cars with this commemorative stamp issued in 1988.

This undated view shows the Newland Coal Company mine near Fayette, West Virginia. If you look closely, you can see a string of waiting railroad hopper cars at the card's far right, just beyond the hillside tipple.

Mines No. 5 and 6, New River Collieries Co., Eccles, W. Va.

This vintage postcard depicts mines No. 5 and 6 of the New River Collieries Company at Eccles in Raleigh County. Located on the Coal River, the mines at Eccles were served by both the C&O and the Virginian Railway. This card was mailed in 1915. Just a year earlier, on April 28, 1914, an explosion killed all 174 miners at work in No. 5 and another nine men in No. 6.

COAL TIPPLE, NEAR WHITESVILLE, W. VA.

This postcard view of the tipple at Glogora Coal Company mine near Whitesville, West Virginia, is undated, but the parked automobiles would seem to suggest the photograph was taken in the 1920s.

MINE No. 1, HOLDEN — ISLAND CREEK COAL COMPANY

Island Creek Coal Company's mine No. 1 in Logan County shipped its first load of coal on the C&O in 1904. The company grew quickly, opening 10 mines within three years and employing thousands of immigrant miners. As it grew, it expanded into Mingo, Wyoming, McDowell, and Fayette Counties.

No 7 AND 8 MINES, HOLDEN, W. VA.

For more than half a century, Island Creek Coal's mines such as Nos. 7 and 8, shown here, would make the company one of the C&O's biggest customers. The company town of Holden, located four miles from Logan, was widely hailed as a model community, known for its tree-lined streets and comfortable, well-kept houses.

Built in 1906, this Island Creek Coal tipple on the Ohio River at Huntington was the last stop for the long C&O trainloads of coal dug from the company's mines in Logan and Mingo Counties in southern West Virginia. In 1907, the tipple handled more than 329,000 tons of coal, transferring it from rail hoppers to river barges. Located just upstream from today's Harris Riverfront Park, the tipple was demolished some years ago. Only the concrete piers remain to mark the spot.

In 1949, Truax-Traer Coal Company introduced a new concept to the coal industry. Instead of cleaning and sorting coal at its eight mines on the C&O's Cabin Creek Subdivision, it sent all the coal directly to this new central cleaning plant built on the Ohio River at Ceredo, just downstream from Huntington.

Here is an undated postcard view of C&O coal pier No. 9 at Newport News, Virginia. In the railroad's earliest years, it shipped coal to many East Coast cities by schooner from Newport News because it was far cheaper than sending the fuel overland. In the years following World War II, most coal loaded here went to overseas markets.

Despite the Depression, the C&O prospered during the 1930s. America still needed coal, and more than a dozen coal trains a day left the yards at Russell en route to the railroad's giant docks at Presque Isle near Toledo, Ohio. In 1935, the C&O invested $1.5 million in new coal-loading facilities at Presque Isle.

June 16, 1923   Car Section   91
RAILWAY AGE

Announcement

Steamship Leviathan ready to leave Newport News

THE same organization whose engineering ability and advanced methods in reconditioning the Leviathan have made her the Queen of the Sea, is also devoting its skill and resources to the building of all types of freight cars and rebuilding locomotives, both to the marine standard of quality.

The advantages of enormous plant facilities, highly skilled American labor and wide diversity of products insure quality production at a reasonable cost.

In addition to building new car equipment, existing types of cars and locomotives will be repaired and rebuilt.

One of an order of 1500 steel hopper cars for the C. & O. Ry.

Newport News Shipbuilding & Dry Dock Company
Newport News   Virginia

In 1886, at the age of 65—an age when most people decide to retire—Collis P. Huntington decided instead to build a shipyard that would be "a credit to our country as well as to ourselves." He christened it the Newport News Shipbuilding and Dry Dock Company and set for it a goal of "building first-class ships." The Virginia shipyard not only built ships of all sizes but also, as this 1923 advertisement attests, railroad cars. The steel hopper car shown is identified as one of 1,500 built by the shipyard for the C&O.

Peach Creek, located about a mile north of Logan, West Virginia, was the principal marshalling yard for the C&O's Logan Subdivision. This 1954 photograph by Gene Huddleston shows a loaded coal train at cantilever signal bridge L617 at Peach Creek. (Courtesy of the C&O Historical Society Collection.)

It's August 1956, and C&O Mallet No. 1506 is shown with a mine run at Logan, West Virginia. An operator is passing up orders to the engineer. (Photograph by Gene Huddleston, courtesy of the C&O Historical Society Collection.)

Doubleheaded H-6 Mallets are shown bringing 100 cars of coal off Piney Creek Branch at Prince, West Virginia, in September 1952. The exhaust can be seen reaching sky high. (Photograph by Gene Huddleston, courtesy of the C&O Historical Society Collection.)

K-4 No. 2752 drifts a coal train into the yard at Russell, Kentucky, in August 1948. Established in 1889, the yard at Russell grew steadily over thee years, eventually becoming the world's largest to be operated by a single railroad. (Courtesy of the C&O Historical Society Collection.)

"All day I watch the coal go by!"

"Train after train. Day and night. Year after year. You wonder where it all comes from and how long it can last."

• • • • • • • •

You're right, Pop, it's a lot of coal—close to half a billion tons a year. Yet, in the more than a century this country has been mining coal, we have used up only a little over one percent of our known supply. 98.8% of the coal that nature put under our soil is still there for future generations.

That is something to think about when you are considering a new heating plant for home or industry. Other fuels will be getting scarce. Every year the wells go deeper. More and more of our fuel oil comes from foreign fields. Growing scarcity can mean uncertain supply and higher relative prices.

Coal you can be sure of. There will be a plentiful supply for many centuries to come. And the price advantage that makes coal a most economical fuel today is likely to grow with every passing year.

COAL — FUEL OF THE FUTURE

Chesapeake and Ohio Railway

Bring your fuel problems to C&O

As the world's largest carrier of bituminous coal, the C&O is intimately familiar with every phase of coal use. We have a large staff of experts who will gladly help you to locate the coal best suited to your needs; to help you use it most efficiently; to help get it to you promptly.

Write to:
Coal Traffic Department
Chesapeake and Ohio Railway
2105 Terminal Tower
Cleveland 1, Ohio

In many of its magazine advertisements during the World War II era, the C&O urged conserving coal as part of the war effort. With the war's end, the railroad's ad writers switched to emphasizing coal's abundant supply (plenty "for many centuries to come") and its affordability. "Coal—Fuel of the Future," reads the logo at bottom left. "Bring your fuel problems to C&O," the advertisement advises.

Six

"The Finest Fleet of Trains in the World"

C&O Train No. 3, the *Fast Flying Virginian*, arrives at Alderson, West Virginia, in July 1967, as the railroad's passenger service enters its final years. E8 No. 4013 can be seen at the head of a three-unit diesel set pulling a 14-car train. The *Fast Flying Virginian*, the C&O's first named passenger train, made its initial run in 1889. (Photograph by Thomas W. Dixon Jr.)

Traveling aboard the nation's earliest railroad cars was a far from comfortable experience. This drawing isn't identified but could well have been the interior of a Louisa Railroad or Virginia Central coach in the years before the Civil War. Some railroads removed the stoves in summer in order to provide more seating. The advent of reclining seats was hailed as a major advance in passenger comfort.

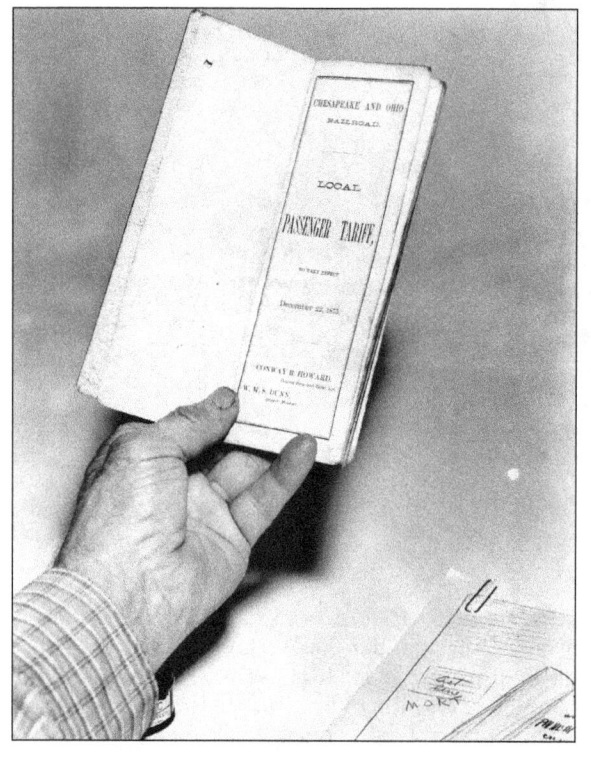

The fledgling C&O of 1875 couldn't have offered much in the way of passenger service, but it was extensive enough to justify printing this booklet of passenger fares. On its creation in 1868, the C&O inherited only a dozen coaches but quickly ordered more as it expanded westward.

This vintage postcard of a C&O passenger train carries no date but a reference in the penciled message on the back suggests it may have been written during the World War I era. The engine is an Atlantic A-16 4-4-2, one of 20 manufactured for the C&O between 1902 and 1916. The study little engines remained in service for decades.

The Pullman Company built combine 200 for the C&O in May 1889. It's shown here at Clifton Forge, Virginia, on January 16, 1915. Although the C&O took delivery of its first all-steel cars in 1911, it continued to operate wooden cars such as this one for a number of years. (Photograph from the collection of Thomas W. Dixon Jr.)

> E. 43.—Special.
>
> **Meeting Grand Lodge of Virginia, A. F. & A. M.**
> TO BE HELD AT
> RICHMOND, VA., DECEMBER 3 to 6, 1901.
>
> TICKET AGENTS
>
> **Chesapeake & Ohio Railway Co.**
> IN VIRGINIA,
>
> Will Sell the Bearer one Excursion Ticket to
>
> **Richmond, Va., and Return,**
> At One and One-Third Lowest First-Class Fare
>
> On any day from November 28 to December 5, inclusive, making return coupon good until December 9, 1901, inclusive.
>
> Good only when bearing official stamp of
> General Passenger Agent.
>
> *N. W. Fuller*
> Gen'l Pass. Agent.
>
> Agents will return these orders to Auditor, with report.
>
> *Not to be accepted by Conductors on Trains.*
> *Void if altered or presented after date stamped.*

Like other railroads of the day, the C&O frequently operated excursions and offered reduced fares to special events. Here a postal reply card announces special fares for riders attending a 1901 meeting in Richmond of the Grand Lodge of Virginia, America Free and Accepted Masons (AF&AM). The fine print cautions that the card will be "Void if altered or presented after date stamped."

Wreck of C. & O. Train No. 3 near Hinton, W. Va., March 12th, 1907.

Train wrecks were a surefire subject for the makers of vintage postcards. This one is captioned "Wreck of C&O Train No. 3 near Hinton, W.Va., March 12th, 1907." Train No. 3 was the *Fast Flying Virginian*. The *FFV*'s cars were steam heated, then a relatively new process. The change eliminated the inherent danger posed by stoves in cars, especially in wrecks.

84

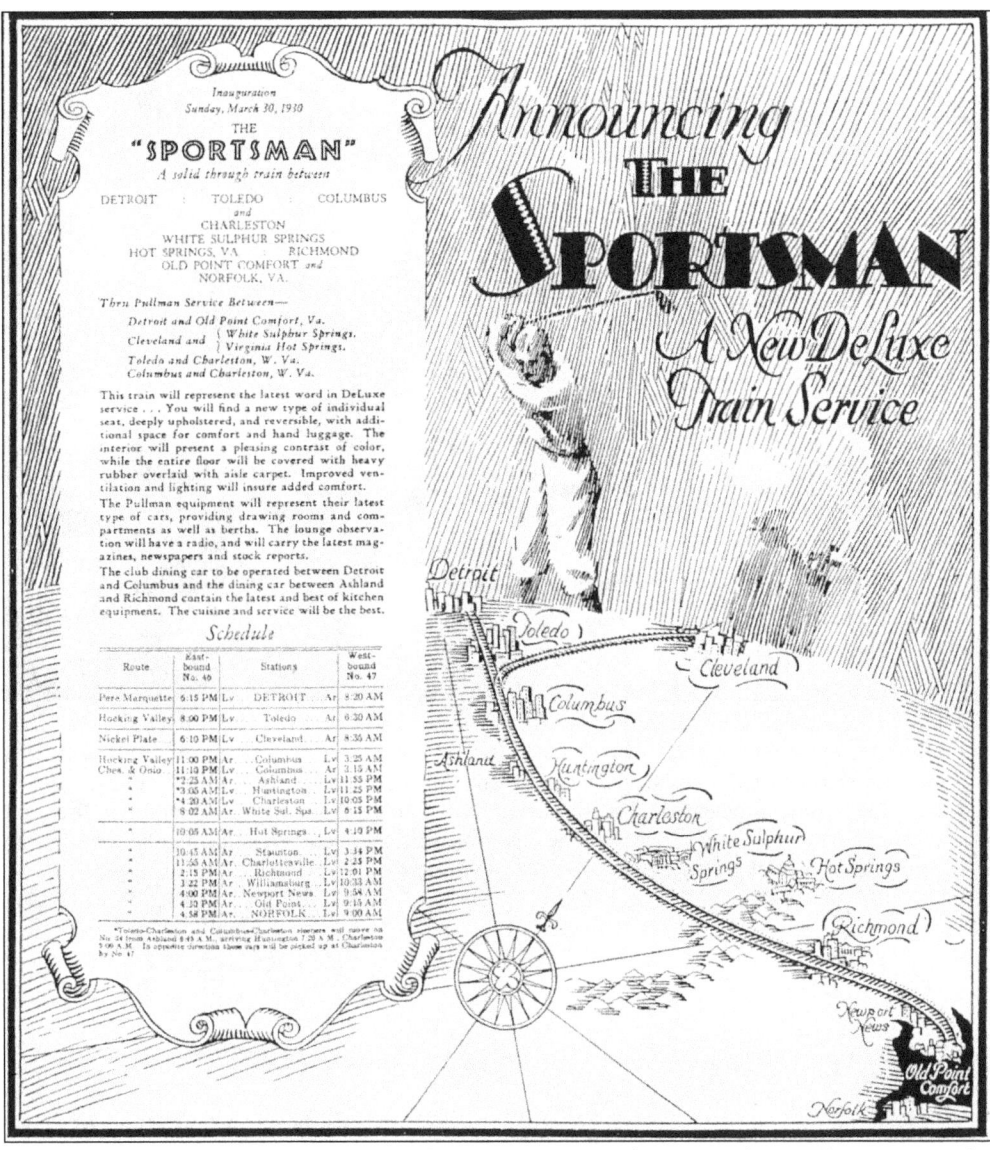

In 1930, in an effort to rejuvenate its slumping passenger business, the C&O inaugurated a new flagship train, the *Sportsman*, designed to link the summer resort areas in Michigan with the seashore resorts of the Chesapeake Bay and Virginia coast. The train traveled the C&O mainline from Newport News, Virginia, to Russell, Kentucky, then headed north on the previously freight-only line to Columbus, Ohio, and over the former Hocking Valley to Toledo, Ohio. Prior to going into service, the new train visited 20 cities in an exhibition run. More than 100,000 people toured the train, including school children let out of class for the big event. (Courtesy of the C&O Historical Society Collection.)

To equip the *Sportsman*, the C&O introduced a new type of coach, called the "Imperial Salon Car." Pullman built 38 of the cars, 30 for the C&O and 8 for the Pere Marquette. All were delivered in 1930. Included was this car, No. 725, now in the collection of the B&O Railroad Museum in Baltimore, Maryland. The cars had plush bucket seats that could be turned to face any direction and other amenities, all at coach rates. The observation/lounge car even had a radio, the first on the C&O. (Photograph by the author.)

Undismayed by the Depression, the C&O proceeded in 1932 to create yet another grand train, this one named the *George Washington* as a tribute to the railroad's "founder." As was the case with the *Sportsman*, motive power for the new train was provided by a spiffed-up Pacific Class F-19, shown here at the Huntington Shops after a 1938 addition of a larger tender. The train name on the tender was lettered on a sign that could be removed if the engine was given other duties.

The C&O ordered no new cars for the *George Washington*. Instead, older cars were given a handsome renovation. In a major innovation, the entire train was air-conditioned, a move that was enthusiastically welcomed by the traveling public. The C&O realized it was on to a good thing, quickly added air-conditioning to the *Sportsman* and the *Fast Flying Virginian* and then heavily promoting that fact. "It's always Springtime on the C&O," proclaimed the cover of this leaflet advertising the air-conditioned trio of trains. The leaflet pronounced the three "The Finest Fleet of Trains in the World."

Reminders of the nation's first president were everywhere on the *George Washington*. The renovated Pullman sleepers were lettered with names of people and places associated with Washington, and the revamped diners were named for Colonial-era taverns. Again, C&O advertisements heavily promoted the presidential connection. "Would the Founder Himself Prefer This Train?" asked this advertisement. Of course the answer was "Yes."

The George Washington

TWO YEARS OLD
and the most talked-of train in the world

In two years The George Washington has established an exclusive identity. Travelers speak of it intimately, as of a friend...a genial companion on pleasure jaunts, a helpful partner on business trips. Its mountain-fresh atmosphere all year 'round, contributed by genuine air-conditioning...its beautifully designed interiors, reminiscent of Mount Vernon...the charm and gracious service of its Tavern cars—these qualities set it apart from other trains, and quickly establish its authentically American character. Yet world travelers also say, and truthfully, that "It has the fleet smoothness of The Flying Scotsman, the sleek beauty of The Golden Arrow, the splendor and comfort of The Rome Express. It is a composite of *all* the luxurious trains in the world." The George Washington, on its second birthday, is a famed American institution.

Any ticket agent can route you on the Chesapeake and Ohio. INSIST UPON IT!

Serving: Washington · New York · Philadelphia · Detroit · Columbus · Toledo · Chicago · Norfolk · Newport News
Richmond · Cincinnati · Louisville · Cleveland · Lexington · Indianapolis · St. Louis · Hot Springs · White Sulphur Springs

FREE TAIL SIGN FOR TOY TRAINS!—*Exact reproduction in full color of sign carried on observation platform of The George Washington. Send 3¢ stamp to cover the cost of mailing—506 Transportation Building, Washington, D. C.*

CHESAPEAKE and OHIO

· 38 ·

This advertisement showing the *George Washington* at White Sulphur Springs gives a good view of the reproduction of Gilbert Stuart's Washington that was on the rail of the platform at the rear of the train's observation car. Interestingly the observation platform itself was strictly cosmetic, as there was no access to it. The advertisement offered model railroaders a reproduction of the Stuart portrait: "Send 3-cent stamp to cover the cost of mailing," the advertisement advised.

88

From the early 1930s on, the C&O was very concerned with public relations. One aspect of that concern was its employee magazine. The magazine changed its name and format several times over the years but was always an award winner. This cover from the September 1937 issue offers an artist's concept of a busy passenger station. The well-dressed young lady is shown studying the season's college football schedules, but isn't that steamer trunk a bit large for a football weekend?

Here's another advertisement promoting summer travel "aboard any of the Chesapeake & Ohio's three fast, air-conditioned trains—*The George Washington . . . The Sportsman . . . The F.F.V.*" The 1938 advertisement promised "the diverting variety of scenery . . . the appetizing meals in the Tavern Car . . . the air-washed, quiet sleeping car that bids you Sleep Like a Kitten." And what C&O advertisement would be complete without Chessie posed in an upper corner?

From a low point of fewer than a million passengers in 1932, the C&O's traffic began a slow but steady rebound, thanks in large measure to the appeal of air-conditioning. The New York World's Fair of 1939 lured many train travelers, but as late as 1940, when this "travel package" advertisement appeared in National Geographic, the railroad was still working hard at drumming up business. That would change virtually overnight with the outbreak of World War II, which saw the C&O move troops by the thousands.

C&O diner "City Tavern" was built by Pullman in 1925. Today it is in the collection of rolling stock on display at the National Museum of Transport in St. Louis, Missouri. Just visible behind it is C&O business car No. 5, originally built for the Vanderbilt family in 1905. The C&O presented both cars to the museum in 1960.

Travelers ordering from this "Chessie Club Service" menu in 1962 could have a ham sandwich for 65¢ and a bottle of Coke for 15¢. If you were traveling through a state that permitted it, you could have a beer (50¢) or a split of champagne ($1.60). The menu included cigarettes at 40¢ a pack.

It's here—a new convenience on the C & O

NO TIPPING

of any C & O employee*

NO TIPPING IN C&O DINERS—THE SERVICE IS COURTEOUS AND FREE

NO TIPPING THE PORTERS IN C&O COACHES—THEIR SERVICES ARE FREE*

Robert R. Young, who became C&O chairman in 1942, was brash, even arrogant, and absolutely determined to shake up the rail industry. Among the innovations Young introduced to the C&O passenger service was, as shown in these cartoons from a 1946 magazine advertisement, a no-tipping policy for C&O employees. "Naturally," the ad noted, "this does not apply to Pullman porters, or to redcaps in union terminals, since they are not C&O employees."

Other innovations Young introduced to the C&O's passenger trains included uniformed airline-style hostesses, the use of credit cards and, as shown here, movies. Despite these efforts, however, passenger traffic continued to decline as travelers abandoned trains, turning instead to air and highway travel.

Still another of Robert Young's ideas was a new long-slung train that would be able to negotiate the curves on existing railroad trackage at high speeds without extensive rebuilding of the track. The project was christened *Train X* and a prototype was built, but when Young left the C&O for the New York Central, the idea went with him. It was reborn on the NYC as the *X-plorer*, but it proved unsuccessful. As envisioned, the light-weight cars would weigh only one-fourth as much as conventional cars, meaning the train would need far less horsepower.

Determined to give travelers a first-class experience they couldn't get on the airlines or behind the wheel of a car, Young envisioned the *Chessie*, a grand new train that would link Cincinnati and Washington, D.C. When the new Budd-built coaches arrived, they were shown off to the press and public at events such as the Chicago Railroad Fair of 1949 (shown here). With passenger traffic rapidly disappearing, the *Chessie* never ran, and most of the cars built for it were sold to other railroads.

This page features two artist's conceptions of what travel would be like aboard the *Chessie*. Here passengers enjoy the scenery as glimpsed from a roof-top lounge. The elevated seating and the large "Vistas Domes" combine to give the passengers what the card describes as "thrilling . . . views of the passing scene."

The tavern lounge car on the *Chessie* would, it was promised, offer passengers "their choice of the dining and lounge section, accented by the illuminated fountain column, or the adjacent snack counter complete with soda fountain."

95

In a burst of post-war optimism, the C&O ordered hundreds of new passenger cars. When reality set in, many were cancelled. Nevertheless, in 1950, the railroad took delivery from Pullman of 59 of these 52-passenger coaches. They would provide the backbone of C&O passenger service until the advent of Amtrak. (Courtesy of the C&O Historical Society Collection.)

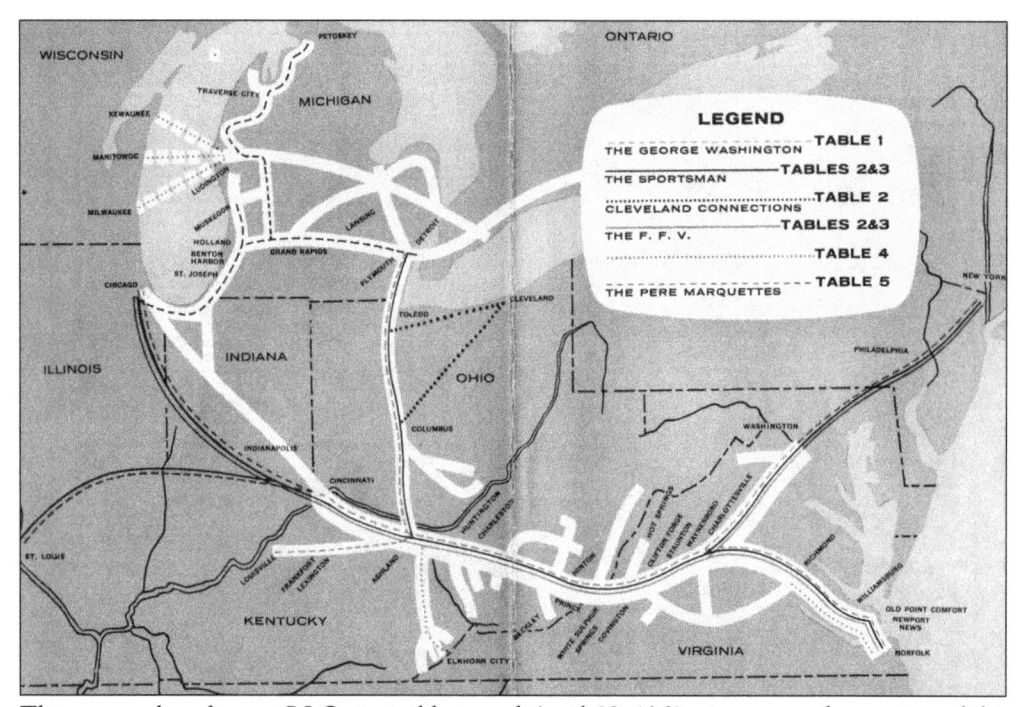

This map, taken from a C&O timetable issued April 29, 1962, gives a good overview of the railroad's passenger routes as it prepared to affiliate with the B&O. By the time Amtrak took over all passenger service in 1971, most of the trains and routes shown here would be memories.

Seven

THE GREENBRIER

By 1827, the James River and Kanawha Turnpike was carrying travelers between Richmond, Virginia, and Charleston, in what is today West Virginia. Many of the weary travelers looked forward to stopping over at White Sulphur Springs to enjoy its mineral waters. This handsome springhouse, a popular landmark on the grounds of the Greenbrier, may have been built even earlier. An 1815 newspaper clipping found within its columns tells about Gen. Andrew Jackson's victory at New Orleans.

White Sulphur Springs soon became a popular destination not just for turnpike travelers but also for well-to-do summer vacationers looking to escape the oppressive heat of the cities. At first they stayed in tents, then later in modest cottages. In 1858, this massive, three-story resort hotel opened with 228 guest rooms and a dining room that could seat 1,200. Officially it was the Grand Central Hotel, but most guests called it "The White" or, in later years, "The Old White."

The Old White had just three summer seasons before it became a military hospital during the Civil War years. After the war it reopened and again attracted visitors in search of rest and relaxation. Gen. Robert E. Lee and his family passed the summers of 1867, 1868, and 1869 at one of the resort's cottages, frequently entertaining guests, as shown in this mural painted for the Greenbrier. The mural can now be seen in the Lee Room at the resort's Presidents' Cottage Museum, which opened in 1932.

The coming of the railroad ushered in a golden age in the West Virginia resort's history. When the C&O extended its line through White Sulphur Springs in 1869, the number of guests at the Old White quickly doubled. Here's a rare view of the C&O's White Sulphur Springs station as it looked about 1903 to 1905. Apparently it was a slow day at the station, as there seems to be little going on.

In 1910, the C&O purchased the Old White, paying $150,000 for it. Three years later, the railway built a modern, Georgian-style building adjacent to it, as shown here. For a few years, the new hotel, christened the Greenbrier, and the Old White operated independently, giving guests a choice between tradition and more modern comforts. At the same time, the railroad built the resort's first golf course. Over the years, the words "golf" and "Greenbrier" would become virtually synonymous. In 1922, the Old White failed to meet a state fire inspection and was ordered demolished.

The C&O not only brought golf to the Greenbrier, it also installed tennis courts, horseback trails, and other recreational facilities, including this enormous indoor swimming pool. The pool actually opened in 1912, a year before the hotel was completed. Responding to demands from guests, the resort set up a polo field. Soon, demand forced the installation of a second field. Fencing, indoor archery, and golf-driving ranges also were set up.

In 1930–1931, at a time when many of the nation's businesses were struggling to survive the impact of the Great Depression, the C&O spent $3.4 million renovating and expanding the Greenbrier. The main structure was expanded from 250 to 580 rooms, a residential wing and an auditorium were added, and the dining areas were doubled. Shown in this vintage postcard is the main dining room.

Throughout the 1920s and 1930s, the Greenbrier was a fashionable playground for the rich and famous, with the truly elite—business barons, Hollywood film stars, and visiting royalty—arriving via private railcars, the era's ultimate symbol of wealth and social standing. Typical distinguished visitors were Crown Prince Olaf of Norway and Crown Princess Martha, shown arriving at the Greenbrier during a 1939 tour of the United States. Here the well-dressed couple poses at the C&O's White Sulphur Springs station after stepping off their private car (just visible behind them at right).

It's Christmas 1939, and a member of the Greenbrier staff is talking things over with an unidentified visitor who must have parked his sleigh at the front entrance. It appears the two are making a list and then checking it twice. Mounted on the wall behind the counter is a reminder of the resort's railroad heritage, an illustrated C&O route map. The map's legend proclaims: "In scenic and historic interest no railroad in American exceeds the Chesapeake and Ohio."

When the country went to war, so did the Greenbrier. In the wake of Pearl Harbor, the U.S State Department asked the resort to house interned Japanese and German diplomats, newspaper correspondents, and their families. Here's a clipping from the *New York Times* of December 20, 1941, reporting on the initial contingent of 150 German internees. Japanese diplomats and correspondents initially were interned at the nearby Homestead. Later they too were housed at the Greenbrier. Ultimately the Greenbrier was home to nearly 1,400 foreign internees.

In this rare photograph taken July 8, 1942, some of the German and Japanese internees can be seen gathering at the White Sulphur Springs station to board a special C&O train to begin their journeys to their home countries. It took six months of difficult negotiations to hammer out the details of exchanging the Germans and Japanese for their American counterparts who been interned by the Axis powers.

Here's another historic shot taken July 8, 1942, at the White Sulphur Springs station as a special train waited to board interned diplomats. Many residents of the White Sulphur Springs area were angered by the presence of the enemy diplomats and correspondents, but as a State Department spokesman pointed out, any mistreatment of those here could spell trouble for the Americans interned by the Germans and Japanese. Despite widespread grumbling, there were no serious incidents.

By July 15, 1942, the last of the foreign diplomats and newsmen were gone, and two weeks later, the Greenbrier reopened for guests, but not for long. On September 1, the U.S. Army took over. Where the State Department had leased the hotel, the army bought it outright and transformed it into a military installation, Ashford General Hospital. Here, wounded servicemen – those in the front row are in wheelchairs – enjoy a musical show in the hotel auditorium.

It's payday at Ashford General Hospital, and some of the hospital's patients, many of them wearing bathrobes over their pajamas, line up to salute and collect their pay. Two military policemen keep an eye on things. More than 25,000 soldiers were treated at the Greenbrier during the army's four years of ownership. The army had agreed in advance to sell the hotel back to the C&O after the war, and at war's end, the railroad held the army to that agreement.

A wonderful *new* Greenbrier will open April 19th

ON APRIL 19TH, The Greenbrier will again open its welcoming doors. You'll recognize the familiar façade, but not the interior, for The Greenbrier has been *completely* restyled and redecorated ... its hospitable personality persists but each of its guest rooms, suites, cottages and public rooms has been given *individual* creative treatment by the noted Dorothy Draper. Visit The Greenbrier, enjoy its unparalleled social and sports facilities. You will appreciate that no effort has been spared to make The Greenbrier the most luxurious, the most enjoyable resort hotel in the world.

The Greenbrier AND COTTAGES
WHITE SULPHUR SPRINGS, WEST VIRGINIA

Accommodations by reservation only · Colorful booklet upon request · NEW YORK 18, 11 W. 42ND ST.—BR 9-6347 · CHICAGO 2, 77 W. WASHINGTON ST.—RAN 0625 · WASHINGTON 5, INVESTMENT BLDG.—RE. 2642

C&O chairman Robert R. Young hired famed decorator Dorothy Draper to restore the Greenbrier's splendor, and she set about doing so, using 30 miles of carpet, 15,000 rolls of wallpaper, and 40,000 gallons of paint in the process. Young then hosted 400 people at a lavish, four-day house party. The VIPs came to the 1948 celebration by limousine, by plane and, of course, by private railcar to see what $12.5 million worth of renovating and redecorating looked like. The C&O took out advertisements in a number of magazines to herald the resort's reopening.

This contemporary postcard view of the Greenbrier's main lobby offers a glimpse of what might be called "the Dorothy Draper" style: black and white chessboard marble floors, big bold flower prints in drapery, fabric and rugs, and elaborate doorway treatments. Draper died in 1969, but the company she founded, now headed by noted designer Carlton Varney, still decorates the Greenbrier. The Greenbrier itself is still owned by CSX, the corporate successor to the old C&O.

The C&O's former White Sulphur Springs station, located just across the road from the Greenbrier, was converted to retail shopping space some years ago. Nevertheless, Amtrack still stops at the old station. Carefully preserved, it looks much the same as it did when private rail cars brought a steady stream of distinguished guests. (Photograph by the author.)

Eight

THE CHESSIE STORY

The C&O had considered using the slogan "Sleep Like a Top" to advertise its air-conditioned passenger trains but quickly changed that to "Sleep Like a Kitten" when L. C. Probert, a C&O vice president in charge of advertising and public relations, chanced on this appealing image of a sleeping kitten. The railroad quickly purchased exclusive rights to the color etching by Viennese artist Guido Gruenewald. It reportedly paid $5 for the rights, surely one of the best bargains in advertising history.

The advertisement where Chessie first appeared made no reference to the name of the kitten, but when the C&O decided to build a whole ad campaign around her, she was quickly named for the railway. In 1934, the C&O printed 40,000 calendars featuring Chessie, and her adoring public snatched up every copy. Subsequent calendars proved equally popular. Today the railway's early Chessie calendars are prized by collectors.

If one cat is cute, how about three? The C&O's 1935 calendar featured not only Chessie but also two smaller kittens. They're shown striking the same sleeping pose as Chessie. (In actuality, they were simply reduced versions of the original etching.) The two were named "Nip" and "Tuck," but over the years their names were seldom used.

The kittens appeared again in this 1935 magazine advertisement, this time actually playing rather than snoozing. Chessie is still sleeping but this time isn't shown in her classic pose. The two young lovebirds in the swing already are planning their honeymoon—including, of course, "a ride on *The George Washington*."

In 1936, Chessie was a mighty busy kitty, appearing in a variety of C&O advertisements, including this one, where's she shown leading "The Big Parade" of passengers to the C&O's trio of named trains. The banner at the front of the parade included not only the "Sleep Like a Kitten" slogan but also identified Chessie as "America's Sleepheart."

109

Also in 1936, Ruth Carroll published *Chessie*, the first of two children's books she wrote about the famous railroad kitten. The sequel, *Chessie and Her Kittens*, was published the following year. Today both books are hard to find and, when located, command premium prices. In the first book, Chessie is a lost kitty, rescued by a C&O train crew and given a new home with young Billy. Here a proud Billy shows her off.

The heart theme was a frequent motif for Chessie magazine advertisements in the late 1930s, including this 1937 advertisement headlined "Heartstrings of Steel." Chessie appears in a heart superimposed over the C&O's double-track mainline. The copy in a facing heart identified the C&O as "the railroad with a heart" and one that's "truly in tune with the travel world!"

110

In an advertisement appearing for Father's Day 1937, "Chessie's Old Man, Father of Her Famous Kittens," finally made his appearance. In an apparent attempt to explain his absence, the ad copy referred to him as "a traveling man," and then quickly added that he did his traveling on the C&O. The creators of the advertisement, again drawing on the name "Chesapeake" for inspiration, christened him "Peake."

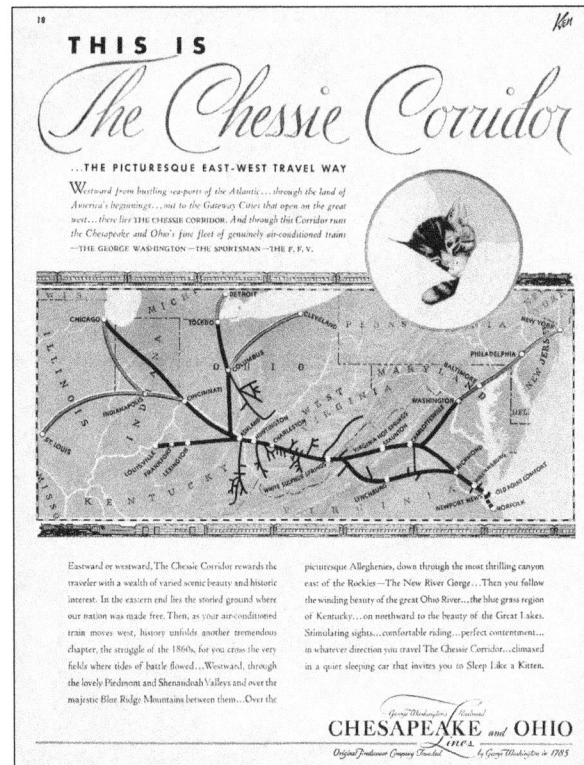

Since her debut, Chessie had promoted the C&O's passenger trains and, to a lesser extent, its freight service, but in 1938, she got a new assignment when her name was applied to "The Chessie Corridor." This was the region served by the C&O and targeted by the railroad's Industrial Development Department to bring in new industry.

111

In World War II, every American was expected to do his or her part, and Chessie and Peake were no exception. Peake enlisted in the army and went off to fight, while Chessie was busy on the home front, helping sell war bonds (as shown in this 1942 poster), promoting civil defense, and calling attention to the contributions to the war effort by the C&O and its thousands of employees.

In this illustration from the 1943 calendar, a sleeping Chessie has made her bed on the floor, giving up her accustomed sleeping-car berth to a soldier. Whereas the prewar era saw Chessie beckoning passengers to the C&O, the war years saw her urging people not to ride unless absolutely necessary so as to make room for traveling soldiers and sailors.

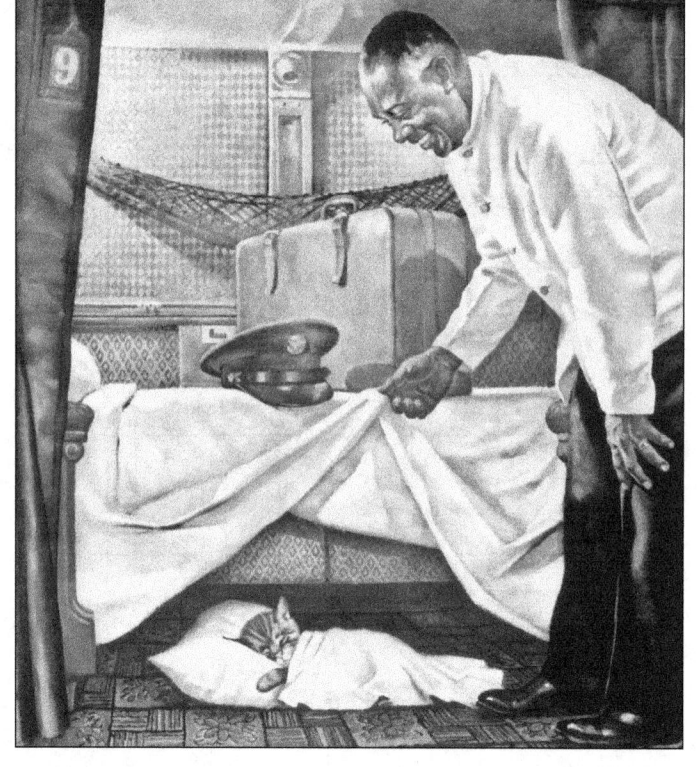

In some of the C&O's wartime magazine advertisements, Chessie was relegated to a supporting role at the bottom of the page. These advertisements focused on the railroad industry's important role in the nation's defense effort. In this 1942 example, two men seated in an observation lounge car spy a passing freight train loaded with military equipment. "There goes Uncle Sam," says one of the men.

Another 1942 magazine advertisement shows a C&O brakeman giving the "highball" lantern signal of "proceed" to a train loaded with wartime supplies as it speeds through the night.

113

The C&O's 1944 calendar featured Peake wistfully looking at a pinup of Chessie. On the floor is a letter from her that he has just read. "Dear Peake," the letter says, "We eagerly await your return from war and here at home we're dong all we can to hasten that day. It's the one thought uppermost in our minds.—Your loving Chessie." The insignia on Peake's cap identifies him, appropriately enough, as a member of the army's Transportation Corps.

The calendar illustration for 1946, "Together Again," showed Peake back home with his family. He's wearing his medals and ribbons and has a bandage on one of his front paws. The kittens look at him adoringly, while Chessie contentedly sleeps away in her favorite berth. Note the souvenir Japanese flag stowed away in the clothes net above.

114

With the end of World War II and the nation's return to a peacetime footing, C&O chairman Robert R. Young planned to introduce a new luxury streamliner named, of course, the *Chessie*. Here's an artist's conception of the train's domed observation car with the name lettered on the side of the car and Chessie's familiar image on the rear drumhead. The post-war decline in passenger traffic doomed Young's dream train.

"Look Chessie, there's The Greenbrier!" This illustration from the 1952 Chessie calendar offered a glimpse of the famed resort at White Sulphur Springs, West Virginia, as it might be seen from a C&O passenger train of that era. Today passengers can enjoy a similar view from Amtrak's *Cardinal* as it travels along the former C&O mainline.

One of the most popular post-war Chessie calendars was this one from 1957, titled "Careful Handling," in which artist Jack Keay rendered a Christmas morning view of a little boy with his new electric train in the background and his engineer's cap perched on the back of his head. As always, Chessie is soundly sleeping.

The last of the classic Chessie calendars, produced for 1959, showed a little girl with a sleeping Chessie on her lap as her train arrived at the Greenbrier. Subsequent calendars issued by the railroad utilized several different formats, including photographs of real cats. Beginning in 1992, CSX authorized the C&O Historical Society to continue the tradition of Chessie calendars.

Nine

LAST LOOK

"IS TWO OVER ONE RAILROAD FARE?" (SIXTEENTH AND DOCK), RICHMOND, VA.

In this closing chapter is a small sample of the varied people, places and things that made up the C&O. What better way to start this last look than with this postcard showing what's said to be the only place in the world where three trunk-line trains may cross each other at the same time and on separate tracks. As the card explains: "At the top is shown a passenger train of the C&O Railway leaving Richmond for the Upper James Valley; just beneath is a train of the S.A.L. Railway leaving the Main Street [Union] Depot for the South, and on the ground [is] a train of the Southern Railway coming into Richmond from West Point on the York River."

The C&O Railway Employee Hospital Association was an important part of the C&O story. The association is credited with being the first prepaid medical organization in the nation and, as such, a forerunner to today's medical insurance. The association was organized in 1897, and that same year saw the first C&O hospital open in Clifton Forge, Virginia, in the former Gladys Inn.

In 1916, the old inn in Clifton Forge was declared a fire hazard and replaced with a handsome masonry hospital building designed by Charles M. Robinson, a prominent architect in Richmond, Virginia. At that time, the railway's employees paid 15¢ to 50¢ per month, depending on their wages, and in return were entitled to "first-class medical attention, medicine, nursing and board without charge."

118

A second C&O hospital opened in Huntington, West Virginia, in 1900. At first, the hospital was located in an old home, but in 1918, it moved into a new red brick building, also designed by architect Robinson. In this postcard view, the old home is just visible at the rear of the new building.

The caption to this 1959 newspaper photograph identifies "Mrs. Charles Stater and Mrs. James Rumbaugh in the record room" at the C&O Hospital in Huntington. By the 1960s, the increasing availability of medical care negated the need for C&O employees to travel far for treatment. In addition, the demise of rail passenger service meant that employees no longer could use free passes to travel to Clifton Forge or Huntington for care. A health care system that had worked well for decades was no longer practical. (Courtesy of The *Huntington Herald-Dispatch*.)

Never one to put all his eggs in one basket, Collis P. Huntington created a sometimes-bewildering network of different corporate entities for his varied enterprises. In 1887, he organized the grandly named Chesapeake and Ohio Steamship Line, which despite its fancy name managed to operate out of this small bungalow in Newport News.

Floods were a recurring threat to the C&O. March 1913 saw flooding all along the Ohio River, and Huntington, West Virginia, was especially hard hit. Hundreds of people were driven from their homes by the high water. The caption on this photograph from a booklet of 1913 flood scenes indicates the small boat pictured is making its way past the United Brethren Church at the corner of Fourth Avenue and Twentieth Street. Note the partially submerged C&O boxcar.

120

The 1916 flood at Cabin Creek, West Virginia, a popular subject with the postcard makers of the day, turned much of the C&O rolling stock at its Cane Fork yard into little more than scrap lumber. The railroad and the nearby coal mines were shut down for a month, with damages estimated at $5 million.

The 1937 flood devastated cities all along the Ohio River, causing untold damages. Here C&O employees in Cincinnati load a portion of 4,000 damaged gas meters for shipment to specialists in Chicago and Erie, Pennsylvania, who could repair them so they would be ready for use when gas service was restored to the stricken area.

This downtown Huntington office building, known as the Coal Exchange Building when it was built, was rechristened the C&O Building when the railway became its major tenet. Later, when the C&O moved out, the building's name reverted to the previous Coal Exchange Building.

In 1926, the C&O spent $3.6 million at its Huntington Locomotive Shop, literally building a new shop around and above the old shop and then tearing down and carting away the old shop. The result was one of the largest and most modern railway shops in the world, capable of rebuilding 50 steam engines per month. Employment at the shop peaked at 3,000 during the 1940s. This undated photograph of a welder at work in the shop appears to be from the 1950s. Today the shop is a state-of-the-art repair facility for CSX diesels. (Courtesy of the C&O Historical Society Collection.)

Coal may be what the C&O is best remembered for, but it was by no means the only cargo the railroad hauled. This advertisement, from a 1951 issue of *Railway Age* magazine, offered the schedules for two daily trains carrying mixed freight. The *Speedwest* operated from Norfolk–Newport News, Virginia, the Carolinas and the Southeast to Chicago and Toledo, connecting with the Pere Marquette there. The *Expediter* traveled the same route eastbound.

Boxcar No. 14337 car displays the "C&O for Progress" logo that was first introduced in 1948 and soon became standard for the railroad's freight cars. As originally designed, the logo included a wavy horizontal line above the word "progress" to suggest a trail of smoke from a steam engine, but in the early 1950s, as seen here, the horizontal line was straightened, a graphic recognition that the railroad was nearing a complete conversion to diesel power.

Built by Pullman in 1905, C&O Business Car No. 5 was one of the oldest cars on the railroad's postwar roster and so was one of the first to go when it started thinning its fleet. The C&O donated the car to the National Museum of Transport in St. Louis, Missouri. The car had three large staterooms, a dining room, and observation room.

C&O Caboose No. 90665, the first Clear View Cupola style, is now on display at the Huntington Railroad Museum, owned and operated by the Collis P. Huntington Railroad Historical Society, Inc. A wooden-bodied caboose that later was steel sheathed, it has been faithfully restored to its original appearance when the C&O donated it to the society. (Photograph by the author.)

This 70-ton covered hopper, built by Pullman-Standard in 1953, was one of several thousand freight cars C&O added to its fleet in the immediate post–World War II years. The new cars, along with the thousands of others added from the Pere Marquette, enabled the railroad to retire many of its older cars that had been given a few years' lease on life by the demands of the war.

The train and auto ferries the C&O operated on Lake Michigan were certainly a far cry from the coal-country scenes generally associated with the railway. The C&O's predecessor company, the Pere Marquette, first offered ferry service across the lake in 1876. At the peak of the service, the C&O operated seven ships, including the *Spartan* and its sister ship, the *Badger*, described as "the world's largest and speediest train ferries."

The ferry *Badger* is show taking on a string of railcars at its homeport of Ludington, Michigan. The *Badger* and the *Spartan* were 410 feet long, had a beam of 59 feet, and cruised at 18 miles per hour. Each could carry 32 loaded freight cars, up to 50 automobiles, and more than 500 passengers. Passenger facilities included dining rooms, a lounge, and private cabins.

Chessietown people "stay put"

That's why many Chessietown industries show records of low labor turnover that would be amazing to employers in other parts of the country. This conservatism and stability shows up in Chessietown's employment picture.

Take Harold, for instance. Harold still lives in the same house his grandfather built. Succeeding generations have added on and modernized it till the old folks wouldn't recognize anything except the view. And the old place, once far in the wilderness, is only a few minutes drive from the paper mill where Harold works as a mechanic.

A man with Harold's background doesn't take a job one day and start looking for another job the next. He believes in repaying fair treatment with loyalty. This human element is one of the many reasons why new industries have been locating along C & O lines at the rate of one every three days for the past several years. Other reasons are nearness to raw materials and quick deliveries to most of the nation's markets.

Let our industrial experts prepare a PIN-POINT survey showing just how these advantages would benefit your particular business. Write to Chesapeake and Ohio Railway, Industrial Development Department, Terminal Tower, Cleveland 1, Ohio. All information is accurate, confidential and adequately supported with photos, maps, aerial surveys and vital statistics.

SERVING: VIRGINIA • WEST VIRGINIA • KENTUCKY
OHIO • INDIANA • MICHIGAN • SOUTHERN ONTARIO

CHESAPEAKE AND OHIO RAILWAY

A tireless advocate for economic development in what this advertisement calls "Chessietown," the C&O frequently hailed the region's advantages in advertisements like this 1953 example in *Fortune*. The advertisement emphasizes the region's stable work force but also gets in plugs for its "nearness to raw materials and quick deliveries to most of the nation's markets." The advertisement manages to even work in a small likeness of Chessie, snoozing away on the "Chessietown" sign.

Visit us at
arcadiapublishing.com

CPSIA information can be obtained
at www.ICGtesting.com
Printed in the USA
LVHW102015211220
674832LV00008B/113